W9-BMU-484

It's all about . . .

CATS AND KITTENS

KINGFISHER
LONDON & NEW YORK

KINGFISHER
LONDON & NEW YORK

Copyright © Macmillan Publishers International Ltd 2018
Published in the United States by Kingfisher,
175 Fifth Ave., New York, NY 10010
Kingfisher is an imprint of Macmillan Children's Books, London
All rights reserved.

Distributed in the U.S. and Canada by Macmillan,
175 Fifth Ave., New York, NY 10010

Library of Congress Cataloging-in-Publication data
has been applied for.

Series editor: Sarah Snashall
Series design: Anthony Hannant (Little Red Ant)
Written by Sarah Snashall

ISBN: 978-0-7534-7411-2

Kingfisher books are available for special promotions
and premiums. For details contact: Special Markets
Department, Macmillan, 175 Fifth Ave.,
New York, NY 10010.

For more information, please visit
www.kingfisherbooks.com

Printed in China
9 8 7 6 5 4 3 2 1
1TR/1117/WKT/UG/105MA

Picture credits
The Publisher would like to thank the following for permission to reproduce their material.
Top = t; Bottom = b; Center = c; Left = l; Right = r
Cover: iStock/Wildroze; back cover iStock/RBOZUK; Pages 2–3, 30–31 iStock/Moncherie;
4 iStock/mussac; 5 iStock/GlobalP, cynoclub; 6 iStock/andreaskrappweis; 7t iStock/
derevlanko; 7b iStock/fotostock_pdv; 8–9 iStock/flibustier; 9b iStock/digihelion; 10 iStock/
guruxoox; 11l iStock/tomch; 11r Alamy/arco images GmbH; 12 iStock/Astrid860; 13t Alamy/
Kathleen Smith; 13b Alamy/Jaguar; 14 iStock/GlobalP; 15t iStock/jehandmade; 15b iStock/
ollikainen; 16 Getty/Jessmyn North; 17t iStock/ollikainen; 17b iStock/smitt; 18 Alamy/
Nature Picture Library; 19t Alamy/Juniors Bildarchiv GmbH; 19 iStock/AlbinaTiplayshina;
20 iStock/seraficus; 21 iStock/castenoid; 21t iStock/AZfotoNL; 22 iStock/fatesun;
23t iStock/maximkabb; 23 iStock/y-studio; 24 Alamy/Juniors Bildarchive Gmbh; 25t iStock/
willopix; 25b iStock/lucielang; 26 Alamy/AFarchive; 27tr Flickr/Jody MacIntyre; 27tl Getty/
Toru Yamanaka; 27br Alamy/Entertainment pictures; 28 iStock/humonia; 29t iStock/
YvonneW; 29 Shutterstock/Tatiana Bobkova; 32 iStock/Sinelyov.
Cards: Front tl Shutterstock/Mr Wichai Thongtape; tr wikicommons/Jason Douglas;
bl iStock/Lightfield Studios; br iStock/Oks88; Back tl iStock/Varvara Kurakina; tr iStock/
Bhanupong Asatamongkoichai; bl Shutterstock/otsphoto; br iStock/Jacqy.

Front cover: A brown and gray tabby kitten plays with a toy.

CONTENTS

We love cats!

We have lived with cats in our homes and farms for thousands of years. Today, there are millions of pet cats in the USA and in Europe. Cats are affectionate, intelligent, and easy to look after.

There are 84 million pet cats in the USA.

FACT...

A group of cats is called a "clowder."

4

There are
73 breeds of cat.

Warm and furry

Cats can have long or short fur. Their fur can lie flat to trap in heat or fluff up to let in cool air. Cats can make their fur stand on end to make their body look bigger.

A cat has four different types of fur:

down — short, soft hair to keep the cat warm

awn hair — to insulate and protect the skin

outer coat — to keep out sunlight and rain

whiskers — to provide information

A Bengal cat has the same markings as its wild ancestor, the Asian leopard cat.

This cat has a calico pattern on its coat.

FACT ...

A dark-gray cat is described as "blue" and a pale-gray cat is described as "lilac."

Whiskers help a cat to know the size of the space around it.

Nose to tail

Just like their wild ancestors, cats are carnivores. A cat's body is well suited to hunting prey.

tail—for balance and communication

FACT ...

Cats can hear very high sounds, such as the sound of a mouse squeaking.

claws—retractable, for climbing and for grabbing prey

8

ears—32 muscles can move in the
direction of the sound

whiskers—for
information
about space and
air movement

eyes—excellent
vision in light
and dark

nose—good
sense of smell

tongue—to lap up milk;
rough for grooming fur

9

Nine lives

It is almost true that a cat will always land on its feet. A cat has a strong balance sensor in its ears and a very flexible spine. If a cat falls, it will turn in the air and land upright. This is called the "righting reflex."

Cats are great at climbing up (but not so good at climbing down).

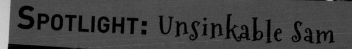

SPOTLIGHT: Unsinkable Sam

Famous for: surviving three separate shipwrecks during 1941

Breed: black-and-white mixed breed

Owned by: German Navy and British Navy

Cats have a great sense of balance.

A cat will twist itself into an upright position as it falls.

Long-haired cats

There are many different breeds of cat. Most cats are a mixture of many different breeds but some cats are "pedigree": they are purebred.

Norwegian Forest cats have very strong claws and are good climbers.

The Maine Coon is the largest domestic breed of cat.

SPOTLIGHT: Tardar Sauce ("Grumpy Cat")

Famous for: being an Internet star with her grumpy, frowning face

Breed: colorpoint mixed breed

Owner: Tabatha Bundesen, Arizona

Short-haired cats

Short-haired cats have . . . short hair! Some, like the American shorthair, have very thick fur. Some, like the Sphynx, seem to have hardly any hair at all.

The Sphynx cat has no fur. Its soft skin is covered in very short hair.

Famous for:	the first cat ever to live in the White House, Washington D.C.
Breed:	tabby
Owned by:	Abraham Lincoln, U.S. President

Oriental shorthair cats have a triangle-shaped head and large, wide-set ears.

The American shorthair is double-coated—it has a thick undercoat of soft fur.

15

Kittens!

For the first week of their life, kittens are blind and deaf; they mostly sleep and drink milk. At two weeks their eyes begin to open and they try to stand. At three weeks their teeth begin to come through and, they can now purr.

A mother cat will usually have a litter of about four kittens.

Kittens will be nursed by their mother for the first six weeks.

FACT . . .

Each kitten's nose is different and unique— just like the fingerprint of a human being.

Growing up

As kittens grow they spend their waking hours learning through play and exploration. They have pretend fights with their siblings. Kittens who grow up together have strong social bonds.

Kittens play to develop their hunting skills.

Kittens form important bonds with their owner through play.

Kittens explore their world—but not always successfully.

Cat talk

Cats make different noises to respond to the world around them. They hiss and growl when threatened, meow or purr when they want something, purr when they are happy, and make a strange chattering sound when excited.

FACT ...

An adult cat will only meow to a human— not to another cat.

When a cat is threatened, it will arch its back and hiss.

A cat showing its belly is relaxed.

A cat will signal its feelings by the way it positions its ears, by opening or closing its eyes, swishing its tail, or fluffing its fur.

A cat flattens its ears when it is scared.

Tall tails

tail up = **alert**

slow tail wave = **cautious**

tail down = **scared or threatened**

thumping or lashing tail = **irritated**

fluffed-up tail = **scared**

tail wrapped around = **relaxed**

21

Cat behavior

Cats sleep for about 16 hours a day and spend half their waking time grooming their fur. Outdoors they will mark their territory, sometimes returning with a "gift" of a dead mouse or bird for their owner.

Sometimes, cats greet each other by rubbing noses and smelling each other.

FACT ...

Cats use smell to recognize their territory. They leave their scent to communicate with other cats.

Cats groom to keep their fur healthy and to calm themselves.

A very old friend

Cats have been keeping us company for over 10,000 years. In the past, cats helped to reduce the number of household pests such as snakes and rats; now they are our companions and friends.

In the Middle Ages people were scared of cats—particularly black ones. As a result, the cat population went down and the rat population rose.

FACT ...

In Ancient Egypt, cats were considered sacred. When a family's pet died, the family would often shave their eyebrows as a sign of mourning.

Ancient Egyptians worshiped a cat-shaped goddess called Bastet.

Famous cats

There are many cats in books and movies, from *Puss in Boots* to the Cheshire Cat in *Alice in Wonderland.* These cats are often made out to be smarter than the other animals around them. In real life, some cats have found fame working for a living.

The fairytale character Puss in Boots is a smooth-talking cat.

The movie *The Secret Life of Pets* tells the story of the pets' antics while their owners are at work.

Caring for your cat

Your cat might seem very independent and might come and go as it wants, but you still need to take care of it—and give your cat lots of affection. You should feed your cat a meat- and fish-based diet and care for its teeth and general health.

A cat door will allow your cat to move in and out of your home freely.

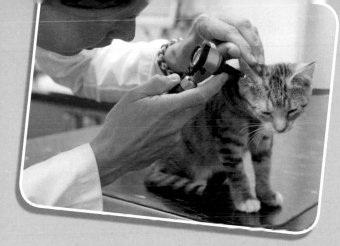

You will need to take your kitten and cat to the vet for its injections and regular checkups.

It is important to play with your kitten so it grows used to people.

GLOSSARY

ancestors Distant relatives from a long time ago.

balance The ability to stay upright and steady.

bond A link of affection.

breed A group of animals that are all the same species and look very similar.

carnivore An animal that only eats meat.

communication Telling others what you are thinking or feeling.

flexible Bends easily without breaking.

grooming Cleaning and brushing the hair with a comb or (cat's) tongue.

intelligent Smart.

insulate To cover and surround something in order to keep warm. Fur keeps a cat warm.

litter A group of kittens all born from the same mother on the same day.

pedigree Having ancestors that are all the same breed.

prey An animal that is hunted by another animal.

reflex An automatic response that you don't have to think about.

retractable Can be pulled back in. A cat can pull its claws back into its paws, unlike a dog.

righting reflex A cat's ability to turn its body quickly when falling so that it lands on its feet.

sensor A device or part of the body that senses something.

siblings Brothers and sisters.

spine Backbone.

territory The area that an animal believes "belongs" to it.

calico A pattern of black, white, and orange splotches on a cat's fur.

INDEX